In 1907 an event took place which clearly established the Rolls-Royce motor car in the forefront of the motoring scene. A 40/50 hp model, designed by Henry Royce and named the Silver Ghost, succeeded in completing 15,000 miles without an involuntary stop – a feat which at that time was more than double the then existing world record.

The Silver Ghost series was given the accolade 'The Best Car in the World' by the motoring press of the time and in this account of Rolls-Royce history, George Bishop describes how the company has striven over the years to maintain its unique reputation.

Henry Royce's motto "Whatsoever is Rightly Done, However Humble is Noble" became the guiding philosophy for generations of engineers from the earliest days to the present. The meticulous attention to detail in engineering, manufacture and design which he insisted upon is evident in each successive model produced by the company as are the qualities of silence, reliability and, as the large number of older models still running testify, longevity.

I, and my present team of engineers at Crewe are devoted to the pursuit of perfection and we are confident that the current Silver Spirit, Corniche and Camargue cars will be worthy successors to the long tradition established by Rolls-Royce. I will leave it to readers to determine for themselves how we at Crewe have succeeded over the years in the face of changes in social and economic conditions.

GEORGE FENN
Managing Director
Rolls-Royce Motors Limited, Crewe.

SILVER SPIRIT

Sir Henry Royce *bottom* built his first car in 1904; despite the placard in the corner, the illustration *below* shows the second example. The car which established the marque's name was of course the silver-finished 40/50 known as the Silver Ghost – a name which was later applied to all 40/50s. The original Ghost is seen *below left and* (in the company of a Camargue, introduced in 1975) *right*. The 1926/27 New Phantom Sedanca Limousine *left* shows the evolutionary process which links the two.

THE FIRST ROYCE CAR
MARCH 31 1904

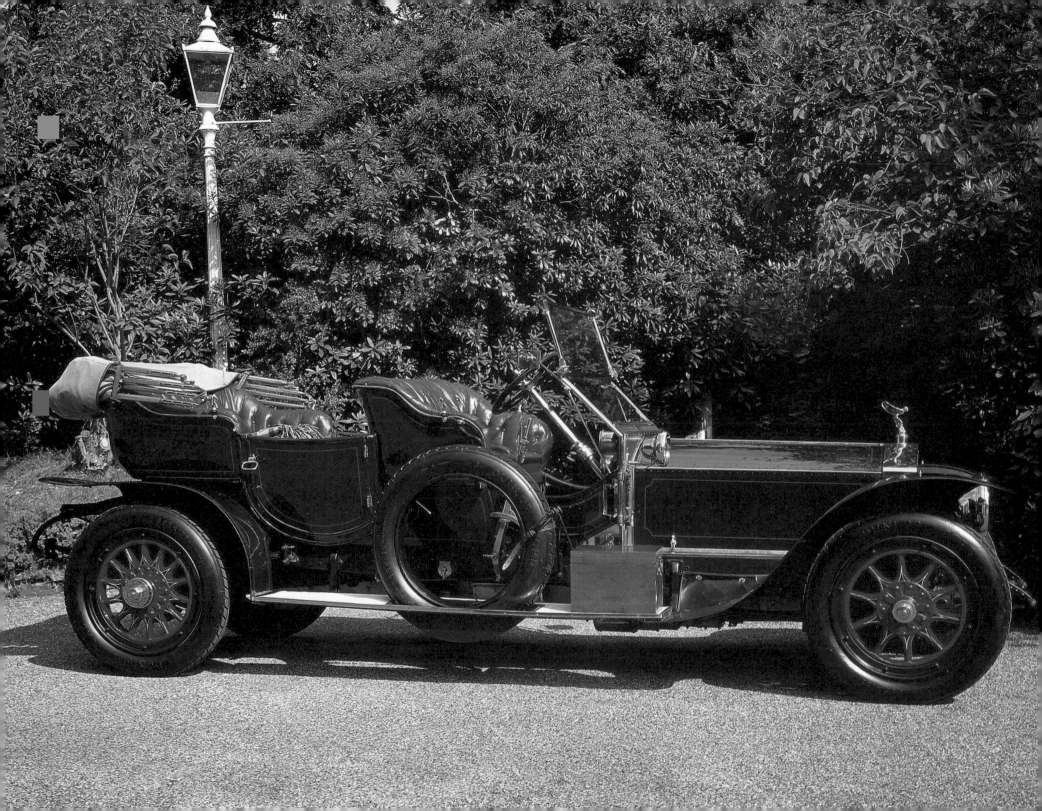

The ten horsepower twin-cylinder Rolls Royce *above* of 1905 was a very good car; but the 1907 Ghost was so nearly perfect that there was little need to change it for many years, as a comparison of AX 201 *top right* with two later Ghosts *above left and facing page* shows. After Rolls Royce took over Bentley Cars, something of the same conservative spirit came to be associated with what had previously been unashamed sports cars *left*.

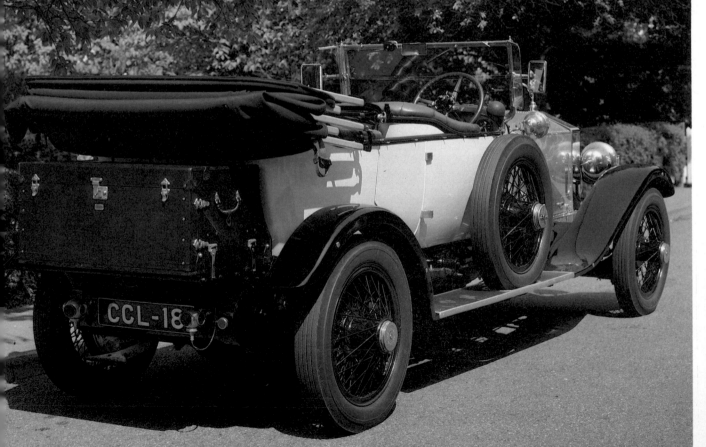

The Silver Ghost chassis was bodied in many ways, from the impressive 1911 cabriolet *above* to the Colonial 1914 model *above left*. Earlier models were often quite sporting, like the 1904 10 hp *below*, but later cars such as the 1925 New Phantom *left* are really rather staid. Sporting motorists preferred something like the mighty Speed Six 6½ litre Bentley *facing page*, built in 1929.

The titanic Hooper Limousine body on a 1912 Ghost chassis *left* recalls an earlier age. Built for space and comfort rather than for speed, it is the epitome of Edwardian dignity. By contrast, the 1916 Ghost landaulette *below* has quite an aggressive look, with a split screen and massive tubular bumper – a common feature on cars for the American market. The Ghost was manufactured until 1925, and the tourer *below left* from that year looks even later – but the chassis and mechanical parts had by then become quite dated.

Facing page: another view of AX 201, whose polished aluminium, silver plating, and aluminium paint inspired the name 'Silver Ghost,' subsequently applied to all 40/50s. From the silver plating on the oil side-lamps *bottom left* to a wooden wedge to hold the clutch out and thus prevent sticking when the car was left *top left*, detailing was extraordinary.

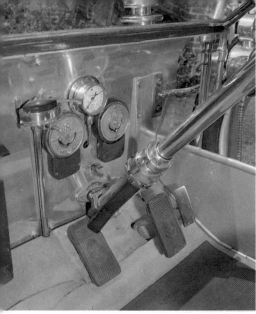

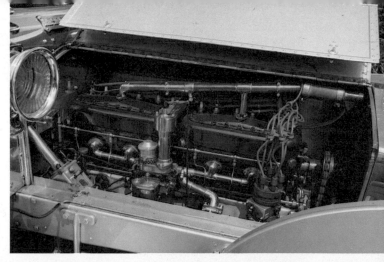

Even the engine was immaculate in polished brass, copper, and black enamel *above, far right*. The controls were simple but beautifully finished; note the conventional pedal layout, at a time when central accelerators were common.

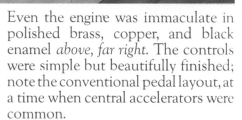

In stark contrast to the considered elegance of the Hooper-bodied 1938 Phantom III limousine and the 1925 Phantom I tourer *below* are the bare, almost brutal, Bentley sports/racers. The legendary 1930 6½ litre and the Blower Bentley *left and above* may have contributed financially to the company's collapse, but racers like the TT model *facing page* enjoyed spectacular success.

A very suave 20/25 from 1931 *left* contrasts disc-clad wheels and smooth lines with the acetylene lamps, accessories and bare springs of a 1911 Ghost *below*.

About 15 years separate the yellow 1923 Twenty *above* and the close-coupled Phantom III *left*, but they represent styles of thought fifty years apart. Custom-built bodies on separate chassis made it comparatively easy to cater for such individual tastes.

The four-seater tourer on a Twenty chassis *left* has such period touches as a rear Auster screen, a metal half-tonneau, and a tyre-mounted rear-view mirror. The other two Rolls Royces *bottom left and below* are American-built: Rolls Royce operated a factory at Springfield, Mass., and built 1703 Silver Ghosts like these between 1921 and 1926. Distinguishing marks include bumpers, indented wheelnuts, and white-wall tyres. On a completely different note was the Blower Bentley *centre left*: compare its functional lines with the rather odd waistline treatment of the car below.

Here again we see the considerable variety of bodies built on the Ghost chassis. The limousines date from 1911 *left* and 1913 *below*, but the boat-tailed two-seater *centre left* was made in 1912. *Above* is a very straightforward touring body dating from 1918, whilst the 1913 model *bottom centre* has a body reputedly designed by Barker but built by Khan in India. *Bottom left* is a very sporting Phantom II from 1931. Only the radiator gives it away as a Rolls Royce.

It was possible to go for the sporting idiom without too much effort. Polished aluminium and the use of bumpers make the Barker-bodied car *left* more sportive, and the V-screen and beautifully-crafted external woodwork have the same effect on the Phantom *above*. The unusual Phantom I coupé *below* has very long lean lines, whilst the slightly gangsterish American-bodied Phantom II *bottom left* has a certain suppressed menace. Even a staid 1911 Ghost limousine *bottom* can be given a vivid appearance with the right paint.

'Colonial' models, like the 1914 Silver Ghost on the *right*, usually had increased ground clearance and beefed-up springs to allow for foreign roads. The Doctor's Coupé was normally ugly but functional; a 1925 Twenty is shown *below*. For looks, the rather sporting 1914 Ghost *above left* or the 1926 Twenty rebodied by Compton in the 'thirties fashion *below left* win hands down. *Above* is a Thrupp and Maberly sedanca body on a Phantom II chassis.

Shown *top left* is Lord Lonsdale's 1923 Twenty with positively reactionary bodywork and *facing page* an utterly classic drophead coupé body on a 1930 Phantom II which would not have looked out of place thirty years later. There was still a wild profusion of bodywork styles, though there is a world of difference between the two sedanca-de-ville bodies *left and above* shown on these pages. Even with quite traditional bodies, some tried dramatic sculptured lines, as witness the wings *below*. Road conditions forced changes, too: the 1939 'overdrive' 4½ litre Bentley *bottom left* was specifically designed for sustained high-speed cruising on the new autobahns.

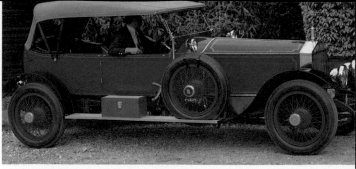

In the early days it was frequently hard to tell 'sporting' cars just by appearance. The very rare 1906 30 hp *below left* and the 1910 Silver Ghost *left* could have put many of their more spartan 'sports' rivals to shame, whilst the rather pedestrian-looking Alpine Eagle *top* was actually a sports modified Silver Ghost, derived from Alpine Trials experience. Later, of course, differentiation became much finer: just compare the fierce-looking red-and-black 'Blower' Bentley *above* with the elegant and refined Phantom I Sedanca *below*.

The massive and astonishingly complex Phantom III, introduced in 1935, was a most impressive car. The 1937 model shown *right* weighs about two and a half tons, but the V-12, twin-plug-per-cylinder engine can bring 90 mph within easy reach – and all very smoothly and quietly. The 1923 Barker-bodied Twenty *below right*, was a more modest vehicle in size, price, and fuel consumption, and was designed to appeal to a rather less plutocratic clientele. Comparing the Phantom III and the Twenty with the 1912 Silver Ghost *below* shows clearly how priorities changed over a quarter of a century, and how the motorcar became an ever more integrated whole.

The photograph on the left sums up the Rolls Royce for many people: past elegance in a pastoral setting. The pictures on the *facing page*, though, give a better idea of what the double-R means to enthusiasts. Everything leads to everything else: the Rolls Royce philosophy is all of a piece. Speed; silence ('at seventy miles an hour the loudest sound is the ticking of the clock . . .'); deep seats and fine materials; luxury; perfect finish; the classically-inspired radiator; money; the Spirit of Ecstasy; elegance; power (sufficient . . .); infinite attention to detail; one could go on indefinitely.

It is easy to forget, though, that a Rolls Royce is not a dream, not a legend. It is a real car, an assemblage of mechanical parts, finely made but ultimately comprehensible. A common gibe is that the Rolls Royce is a triumph of engineering over design, but after all, the word has entered the language. We call a Leica the Rolls Royce of cameras, a Brough Superior the Rolls Royce of motorcycles. Or, as Rolls Royce themselves once advertised their product, 'The Rolls Royce of Cars.'

SILVER SPIRIT

An outbreak of heresy: the 1939 'over-drive' Bentley *below* is easily the best-looking car on this page. The bilious and bulbous Ghost *bottom left* dates from 1913, but looks later, whilst the 1927 Phantom I *left* and the 1935 20/25 *above* lack originality – at least from these angles.

The 'letter-box' windshield of the Phantom III *below* helps to disguise its vast size – a popular trick in the 1930s – and gives it a much more modern and rakish look than the 1928 Phantom I *right* which is, after all, only a very few years older. Then again, consider how fashions change nowadays . . .

The Silver Ghost *right* shows the difficulty of ascribing American origins to a Rolls Royce. The substantial bumper and the whitewall tyres point across the Atlantic, but the hubs are of conventional (i.e. British) design and the Auster screen was fitted both for the home market and for export to the Colonies. Note the horizontally slatted radiator and the massive cylindrical lights – a favourite with the American market. There is a transatlantic influence here, certainly.

On these pages, we have the two different faces of Rolls Royce. The Phantom III *facing page* is the epitome of respectability and orthodoxy; its vast size is to a considerable extent disguised by its beautifully integrated design. It was almost impossibly expensive to produce, and appealed principally to the very very rich. The bodywork is undoubtedly one of H.J. Mulliner's finest achievements.

The Phantom *top right* hails from Springfield – note the bumper, tyres, hubs, and headlights – and is about as near to a personal runabout as you can decently put on a Phantom chassis, while the red Twenty *right* is actually a rebodied 1926 Twenty. The amazing boat-style body *above* is on a three-litre Bentley chassis, but similar coachwork appeared on Rolls Royces.

Sheer elegance, albeit in a wide variety of body styles, is the keynote here. The 1933 Phantom II faux cabriolet *left* is a particularly stunning car in the 'thirties fashion – but visibility must have been appalling. The 1930 sports cabriolet de ville *bottom left* is scarcely less impressive; a long wheelbase always makes the coachbuilder's job easier, though there is a hint of Teutonic massiveness in the blue Phantom II drophead coupé *centre left*. By 1939, when the Mulliner-bodied Mk. V Bentley *facing page* was made, even Bentleys were elegant rather than sporting.

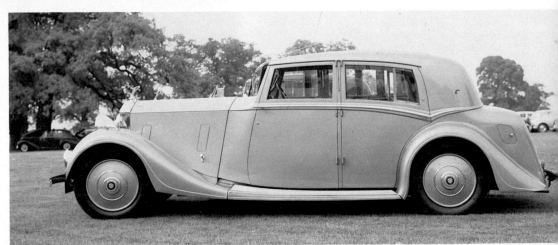

With Bentleys, there were always people who cared more about 'go' than about 'show'; the rather odd two seater *facing page* was obviously built with the former in mind. Often, though, the two went together, as witness the two Bentleys shown *below*. Occasionally, you get neither: the 1935 20/25 sedanca de ville *left* was not particularly quick and looked distinctly peculiar, but the balance is redressed somewhat by the Phantom III on the *right*.

Once again, Bentley steals the honours: the 1955 R-type Continental *facing page* is very beautiful; the Phantom VI *right* is merely very big.

The Bentley R-type Continental *facing page* may only have had six cylinders; but then, so did the Silver Ghost *bottom right* over forty years previously. More modern Rolls products use the ubiquitous V8, whether in the guise of the Bentley *right*, the Phantom VI *bottom*, the Corniche convertible *below*, or the Silver Wraith *centre right*. It is interesting to speculate upon what part fashion plays in engineering; many American manufacturers are returning to the straight six, whilst Jaguar prefer a modern version of the V12.

Rolls did not immediately change the character of the Bentley; the special-bodied model *below* dates from 1933. Nowadays the Camargue *bottom left* can outperform any sports car of the 1930s.

The Silver Dawn *top* is the Rolls Royce variant of the standard steel Mk. VI Bentley; similarly, the Bentley Mulsanne *bottom right* is a Silver Spirit with a Bentley radiator. The Silver Dawn/Mk. VI looks quite similar to the contemporary coach-built Wraiths *above and below*. Somewhat improbably, the two Phantom IIIs *facing page top left and right* look smaller than the formal 20/25 *top right* – a triumph of coachbuilding.

Five cars – but less different than you might think. All use the ubiquitous V8 engine: only the Phantom IV, built exclusively for royalty and heads of state, uses a straight-eight. The Phantom VI *bottom right* is the largest car to use the V8 and appeals to a very special market indeed; with a price of about £100,000, it must do. It has such refinements as dual air conditioning systems, one for the chauffeur and one for the passengers, and is built to the buyer's requirements. For those who still want size and comfort, though with a rather more modern body shape, there is the Silver Spur *facing page top left*; this is a long-wheelbase version of the Silver Spirit.

The Silver Shadow is, perhaps, the definitive modern Rolls Royce – and certainly one of the most popular and successful models. The car illustrated here is a 1977 Shadow II *facing page bottom left*. To varying degrees, all subsequent Rolls Royces have been derived from it, the Corniche *this page* and the Silver Spirit *facing page top right* among them. Of course, innovation is constant, and revisions to the suspension and steering geometry when the Silver Spirit appeared made it the best-handling Rolls Royce to date.

Overleaf is a 1978 Corniche convertible – referred to by the company as 'the ultimate personal Rolls Royce' – and a kaleidoscope of manufacturing processes: lowering the body onto the mechanical components and sub-frames; balancing the engine; matching veneers; fitting the gearbox to the engine; hand-soldering the famous radiator. Rolls Royce have always aimed to combine the best of old-fashioned craftsmanship with the latest engineering techniques. They are quite willing to buy in the best designs: the gearbox is a Borg Warner design, built under licence by Rolls Royce.

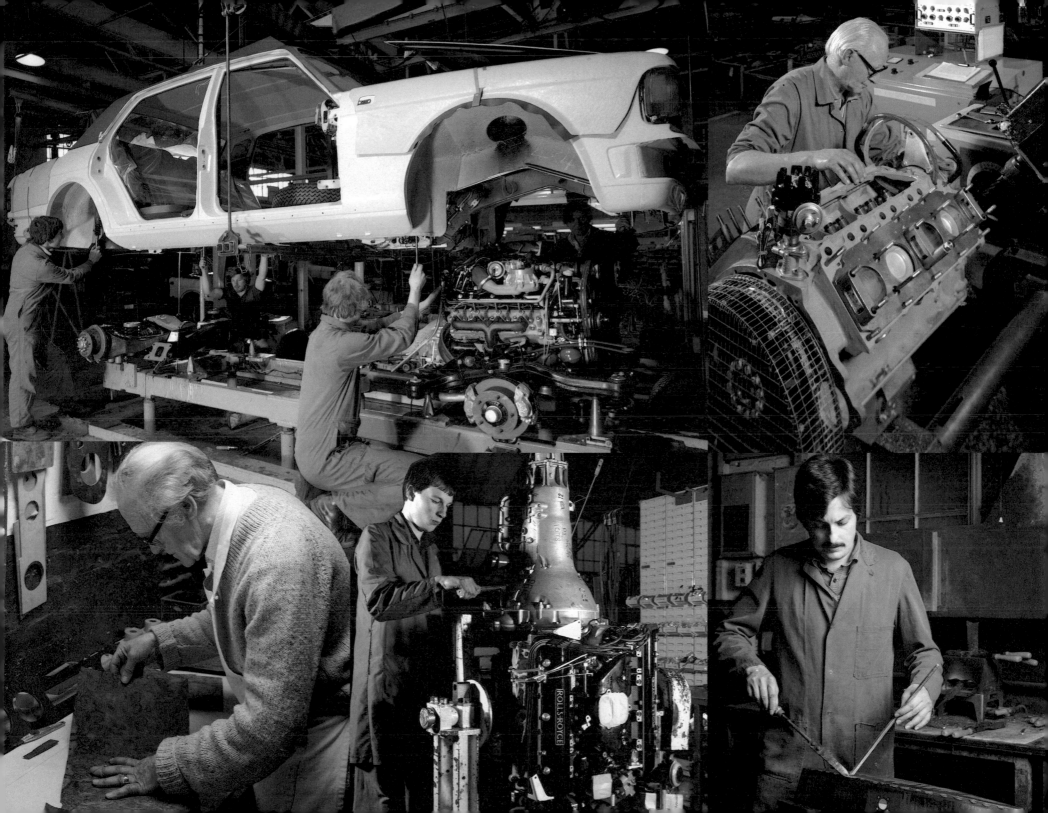

Corniche and Camargue; one name redolent of the 'twenties and 'thirties, the other of the 'seventies and 'eighties – but both very fine cars. Traditionalists will perhaps prefer the Corniche *below and top right*, but the Carmargue *above and bottom right* has its advocates.

Every new Rolls Royce upsets the traditionalists, and the Silver Spirit was no exception. It is an interesting exercise to cover the radiator of the car on the *facing page centre right* to see how much truth there is in the gibe that it is the best Mercedes Rolls Royce ever built; certainly, a Silver Spirit with the radiator removed for photographic purposes was mistaken by three casual visitors to the studio for a Stuttgart product.

On the other hand, as the car on *this page* shows, there is still a certain lordliness to the Rolls Royce which few if any other cars have ever managed to emulate. There is more to it than just a pretty radiator, though. Under the skin of the Silver Spirit lies the fruit of around eighty years' experience of building first-class motor cars, very nearly regardless of cost. No other maker of cars of this quality has survived so long; no other maker of such long standing has made such cars so consistently.

Overleaf: a Camargue and a Silver Spirit. The last picture in the book, though, is a 1926 Twenty, with open tourer bodywork by Barker.

Dep. Leg. B. 21.927/83

© 1983 Colour Library International Ltd.
First published in the USA 1983 by Exeter Books
Distributed by Bookthrift
Exeter is a trademark of Simon & Schuster, Inc.
Bookthrift is a trademark of Simon & Schuster, Inc.
New York, New York.
Printed by Cayfosa, Bound by Eurobinder, Barcelona, Spain
All rights reserved
ISBN 0-671-06251-4